# THE BEATLES

TRIUMPH
ENTERTAINMENT
Division of Triumph Books
601 South LaSalle Street
Chicago, Illinois 60605

# THE BEATLES

THE BEATLES

# THE BEATLES

BEATLES 7

**John Delavan**
Executive Editor

•

**Elliott From**
Creative Director

•

**Brendan O'Neill**
Editor

•

**Melanie Wolkoff**
Assistant Editor

•

**Stacy Lipner**
Photo Editor

TERENCE SPENCER/RETNA LTD.

THE BEATLES

# CONTENTS

# ALL YOU NEED IS LOVE:

# THE STORY OF THE BEATLES

JUST MENTION THE "FAB FOUR" AND WORLDWIDE RECOGNITION IS IMMEDIATE.

NO LAST NAMES NEEDED HERE. EVERYBODY KNOWS PAUL, JOHN, GEORGE AND RINGO.

BY DAVID FANTLE AND THOMAS JOHNSON

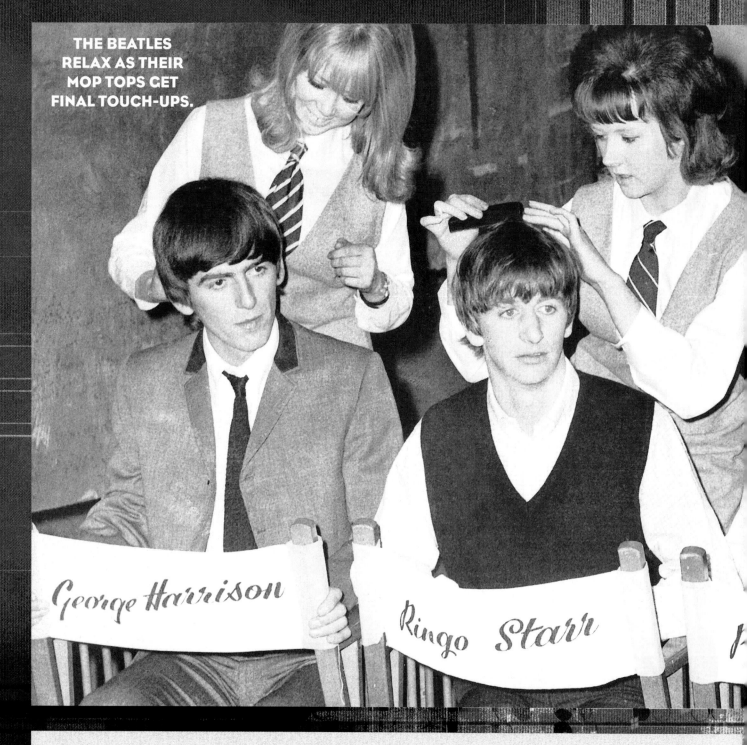

THE BEATLES RELAX AS THEIR MOP TOPS GET FINAL TOUCH-UPS.

*George Harrison*

*Ringo Starr*

**A**rguably, no other group has done more to change the pop music landscape during the last century than the four lads from Liverpool. The Beatles almost single-handedly revolutionized rock 'n' roll music. It has been 30 years since the group disbanded and 20 years since John Lennon was shot to death, but the music plays on, and legions of new fans are swaying to their timeless beats and poignant lyrics.

Now, with the release of "The Beatles Anthology," legions of new fans will be exposed to The Beatles and the group's story.

## THE BEATLES RULE

Talk about longevity! Forget Britney Spears, *NSYNC and Backstreet Boys. The Beatles still rule. According to July 2000 figures from the Recording Industry Association of America, The Beatles have six albums that have recently hit new multiplatinum levels (sales of more than 1 million each). The "White Album" led all albums with 18 million copies sold, making it one of the seven highest certified albums

of all time. Following close behind are "The Beatles 1967-1970" at 15 million, "The Beatles 1962-1966" at 14 million and "Love Songs" at 3 million. The July certifications bring The Beatles' total album sales up to 113.5 million units, cementing their position as the highest certified artists in history.

The Beatles not only reinvented and redefined rock 'n' roll, they supplanted the uniquely American popular music genre, including its primary interpreters such as Frank Sinatra, Perry Como, Tony Bennett and Dean Martin. They also switched the music industry's emphasis to groups rather than individual rock 'n' roll acts such as Elvis Presley, Little Richard, Buddy Holly, Chuck Berry and Jerry Lee Lewis.

They were the original trendsetters that spawned other legendary groups such as the Rolling Stones and The Who in England, as well as the Beach Boys in the United States.

The Beatles' place in music history was not the result of some "master plan." It was more a harmonic convergence that brought these ☞

four unique artistic temperaments together as a band.

"We used to sort of think of things in stages," Paul McCartney told David Frost in a 1964 interview. "When we first started off, playing in The Cavern, I thought first of all, 'Let's get a record contract.' We all did. When we got a record contract, we said, 'Let's get a number one hit.'

… Got one of them."

"From our earliest days in Liverpool, George and I on the one hand and Paul on the other had different musical tastes," John Lennon said about the musical differences that often engendered heated debate among members of the group. "Paul preferred 'pop type' music and we preferred what is now called

'underground.' This may have led to arguments, particularly between Paul and George, but the contrast in tastes, I'm sure, did more good than harm, musically speaking, and contributed to our success."

But long before international success, the road to stardom started off on a bumpy note for the four men from Liverpool.

## LIFE IN LIVERPOOL

The roots of The Beatles can be traced to Liverpool, England, in the late 1950s. The rage at the time in Britain was called skiffle — jazz or folk music groups comprised of members who play unconventional instruments such as jugs and washboards.

Inspired by this craze, John Lennon (born John Winston Lennon) purchased a guitar and in March 1957 formed a skiffle group called The Quarryman, named after his high school, Quarry Bank. The band members changed frequently, but by October 1959, the group consisted of Lennon, his younger classmate Paul McCartney (born James Paul

McCartney), George Harrison and drummer Colin Hanton.

Lennon's art school classmate, Stuart Sutcliffe, joined the band on bass in March 1960. After a brief stint as Johnny and the Moondogs, the group changed its name to The Beetles, in response to Buddy Holly's group, The Crickets. By that summer they were renamed The Silver ☞

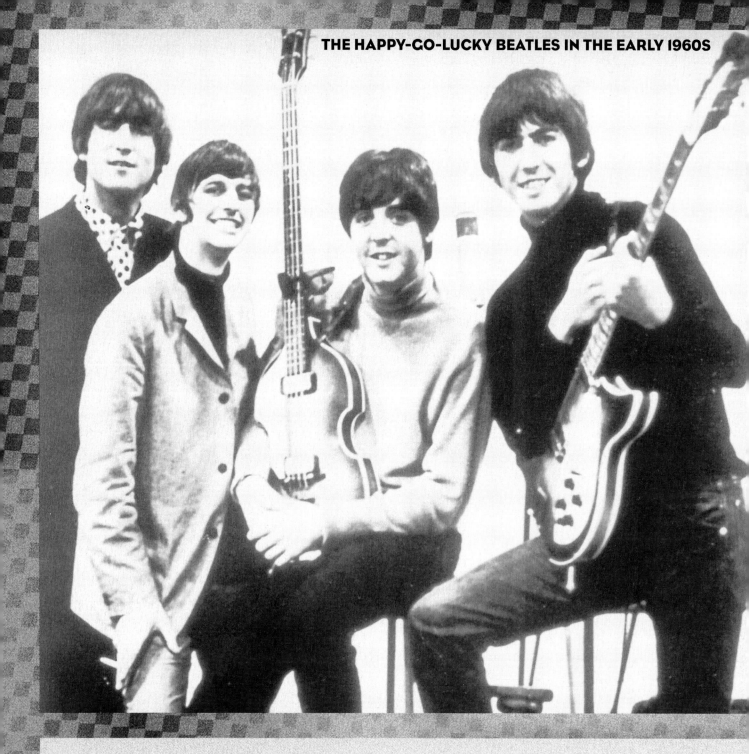

Beatles, and finally they settled on just The Beatles in August 1960. Other popular Beatles' lore suggests that Lennon came up with the name when "a man in a flaming pie appeared and said, "You shall be Beetles with an 'A.' "

With the name now set, the group recruited a new drummer, Pete Best, and departed for Hamburg, West Germany, to take a shot at European stardom. The band became a popular local act and played extended gigs at Bruno Koschminder's Indra Club. During this period, the group often played grueling six-hour sets and the historic musical collaboration between Lennon and McCartney began to take root.

What also took shape during this period was the group's signature "mop top" or bowl-cut hairstyles, the creation of Sutcliffe's German fiancée, Astrid Kirchherr. Just as The Beatles' popularity was growing, the German trip ended abruptly in December 1960, when Harrison was deported for being underage and the others lost their work permits. During the tumult, The Beatles dismissed

**THE BEATLES ALWAYS ENJOYED PERFORMING LIVE.**

manager Allan Williams, who booked many of their early appearances.

The Beatles regrouped back home and performed several times at The Cavern Club in Liverpool. The group returned to Germany in early 1961 and played backup for singer Tony Sheridan on the single "My Bonnie" as well as other songs. These sessions were later released in the mid-1960s and deceptively marketed as "new" Beatles material.

While in Germany, Sutcliffe decided to leave the band and remain in the country to pursue a painting career. McCartney, a more accomplished musician, moved to the bass guitar spot. Tragically, Sutcliffe died on April 10, 1962, of a brain hemorrhage. He was 21 years old.

After their days in Germany, The Beatles returned and played clubs throughout England, with a home base at The Cavern Club. Because of requests from customers for the "My Bonnie" recording, Brian Epstein, manager of a North End music store, became interested in the group and by the end of the year assumed management duties. ☞

## FOR THE RECORD

As manager, Epstein's first priority was to land the group a recording contract, but this was easier said than done. On January 1, 1962, The Beatles auditioned for Decca Records, performing 12 covers and three original songs. The band was rejected, told that "guitar groups are on the way out." Other labels took a look, but passed. Their fortunes changed in May 1962, when The Beatles found a fan in EMI producer George Martin. After auditioning for EMI subsidiary Parlophone, the group signed a recording contract on May 9.

After a few recording sessions, Martin expressed displeasure with drummer Pete Best. Best was fired from the group and replaced by a well-known local drummer, Ringo Starr (born Richard Starkey).

Although considered a superior drummer, Starr had misgivings about his talents.

"I started to be an engineer, but I banged my thumb on the first day," he said. "I became a drummer because it was the only thing I could do.

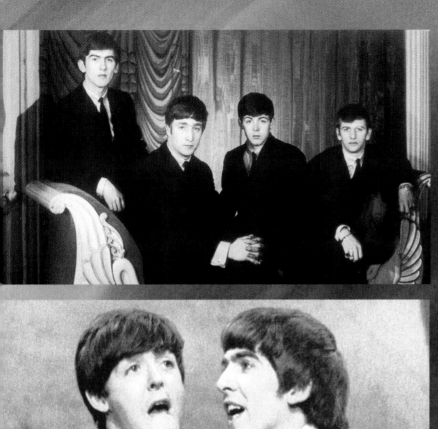

But whenever I hear another drummer, I know I'm no good. I can only play on the offbeat because John can't keep up on the rhythm guitar. I'm no good on the technical things, but I'm good with all the motions, swinging my head, like. That's because I love to dance, but you can't do that on the drums."

By the end of 1962, The Beatles' first single, "Love Me Do," was a top 20 hit in England. A master promoter, Martin allegedly helped sales by gobbling up 10,000 copies of the single to ensure chart status. The band began making regularly scheduled guest appearances on the BBC, performing more than 50 times between 1962 and 1964.

In February 1963, The Beatles returned to the studio to record 10 new songs for their first album, "Please Please Me." Amazingly, all 10 tracks were recorded in a day, and the album was released the following month. Appearing in front of 6 million viewers on the U.K. program *Thank Your Lucky Stars* to promote the single, the title song and the band became an overnight ☞

sensation. The song stayed at No. 1 in England for 30 weeks, and by October screaming fans (mostly female) jammed each live performance. The press dubbed this phenomenon "Beatlemania."

"Please Please Me" was soon followed by other hits, including "From Me to You," "She Loves You" and "I Want to Hold Your Hand."

After an early November performance before the royal family, Parlophone released a second Beatles album, "With The Beatles." By the end of 1963, the group's album sales had hit 2.5 million in Britain alone.

## THE BRITISH INVASION

Success at home was fine, but The Beatles knew they had to cross the Atlantic and make it in America in order to become true international superstars. Working against the group was the fact that EMI's U.S. partner, Capitol, refused to issue the first few Beatles singles in the United States. The songs were picked up by indie label Vee Jay, which packaged the singles into their first U.S. LP, "Introducing The Beatles." ☞

**THE LEADERS OF 'THE BRITISH INVASION' ADOPT A MORE FORMAL LOOK.**

**THE BEATLES POSING OUTDOORS, FROM 'THE BEATLES ANTHOLOGY' VIDEO**

PAUL, GEORGE, JOHN AND RINGO
GET CRAZY FOR THE CAMERA.

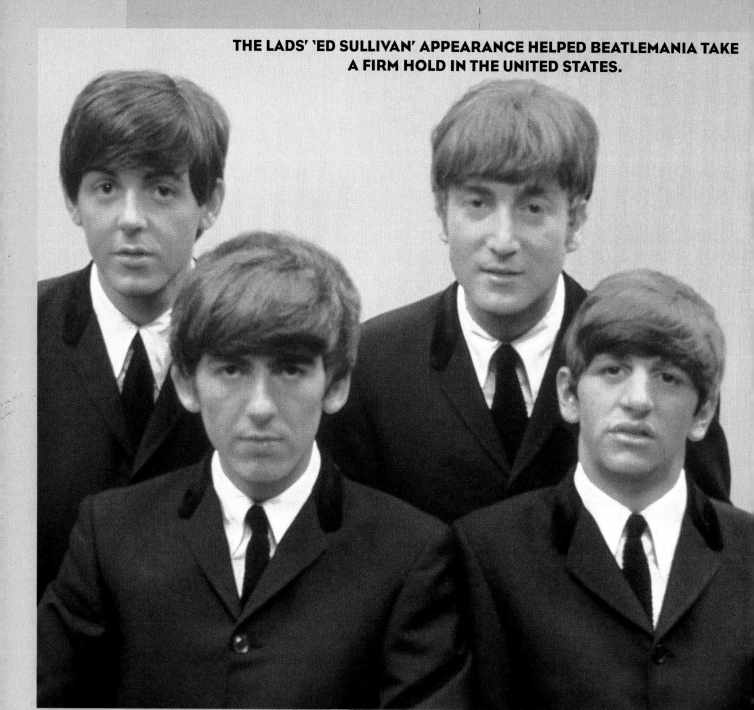

**THE LADS' 'ED SULLIVAN' APPEARANCE HELPED BEATLEMANIA TAKE A FIRM HOLD IN THE UNITED STATES.**

Despite lacking the marketing muscle of a major record label, the material enjoyed brisk sales in America during the second half of 1963. After some legal haggling, the courts in 1964 awarded EMI/Capitol the rights to all Beatles recordings.

In January 1964, Capitol released its first U.S. Beatles LP, "Meet The Beatles." The new record consisted of material culled from the group's two British albums.

Ed Sullivan was as unhip as they come, but on his top-rated Sunday night variety show on CBS, *The Ed Sullivan Show*, he would sacrifice his own personal tastes in favor of high ratings. His trademark line, "really big shoe," became fodder for comics during that period. The stiff-as-a-board Sullivan was savvy enough to book The Beatles for a three-weekend stint in February 1964.

The band's rendition of "I Want to Hold Your Hand" caused near hysteria from the mostly female studio audience. An astonishing 73 million people viewed the program, and "Beatlemania" took firm hold in the United States. ☞

THE BEATLES HANG OUT
WITH ED SULLIVAN IN 1964.

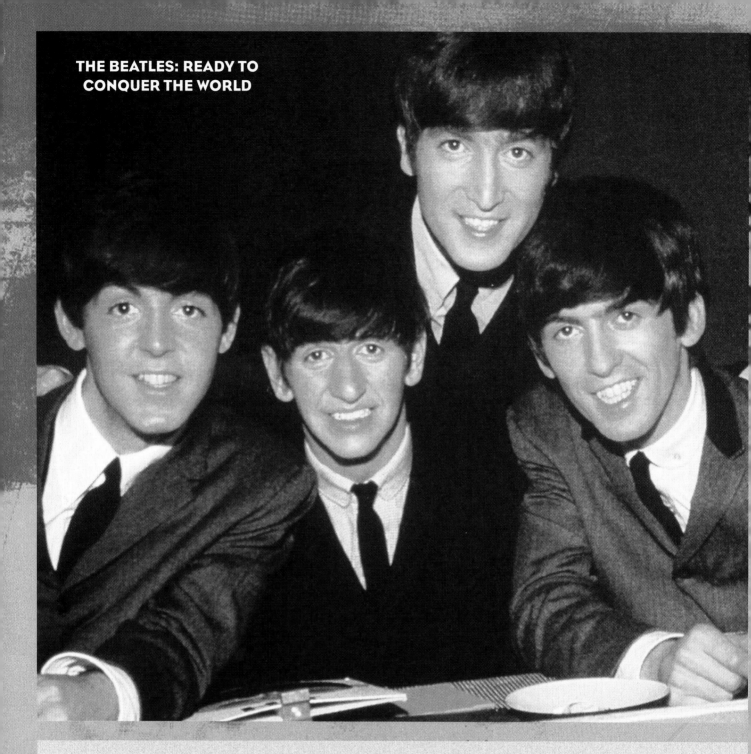

By April, they held the first five places in the Billboard Hot 100, and north of the border in Canada, they boasted nine records in the top 10.

Beatlemania also prompted a marketing boom for the group. Everything from Beatles badges and dolls to chewing gum and breath mints reflected the group's merchandising power.

"Being able to do things that you enjoy doing, you get a bit of power when you reach a certain stage. And then you can suggest things that you want to do," McCartney said when asked by David Frost what was the best thing about being a Beatle. "I mean, we can turn to Brian (Epstein) and say, 'Could we do such and such a thing … like a film?' And he'll say,

'Well, I'll try and fix it boy.' He's good like that you know."

The Fab Four had put the Liverpool sound on the map and the beat had spread to the United States. The Beatles, like their American parallel, Bob Dylan, showed the world that pop music could be more than a bubblegum trifle quickly digested and forgotten by hordes of

screaming teens.

From their earliest days, The Beatles insisted on composing much of their own material, a departure from past industry practices. The group did cover songs written by others, including Chuck Berry, Buddy Holly, Carl Perkins, Bacharach and David and Leiber and Stoller.

Over time, Lennon and McCartney became so prolific that they began providing songs to other artists, most notably the Rolling Stones with their second single, "I Wanna Be Your Man." In fact, the members of The Beatles often encouraged their English competitors to write their own songs in order to collect the lucrative royalties that came with ownership.

## THE BIG SCREEN

Capitalizing on their success on the recording charts and their appearances on Ed Sullivan, The Beatles starred in the hit Richard Lester-directed comedy film, *A Hard Day's Night*. A critical and commercial success, the film spawned a hit soundtrack recording. Following the release ☞

GEORGE, PAUL AND JOHN GRAB SOME DINNER IN AUSTRALIA IN 1964.

of the movie in July 1964, the band embarked on its first North American tour, packing stadiums on 25 dates in the United States and Canada.

In 1965, the band appeared in the comedic James Bond spoof "Help," which produced another hit soundtrack followed by a successful tour. The year ended with the release of their first double-sided No. 1 single, "We Can Work it Out" and "Day Tripper."

For Christmas 1965, The Beatles treated their fans to a remarkably diverse collection of songs in the album "Rubber Soul." The tracks ranged from the pointed satire of "Nowhere Man" to the introspective "In My Life."

The prolific group was cranking out recordings at a torrid pace at the bequest of EMI (part of the company's plan to release a new Beatles album every six months.) So in June 1966, the album "Yesterday… And Today" was released. To make a statement, the album featured a shocking cover of the Fab Four surrounded by raw meat and butchered baby dolls, a protest of

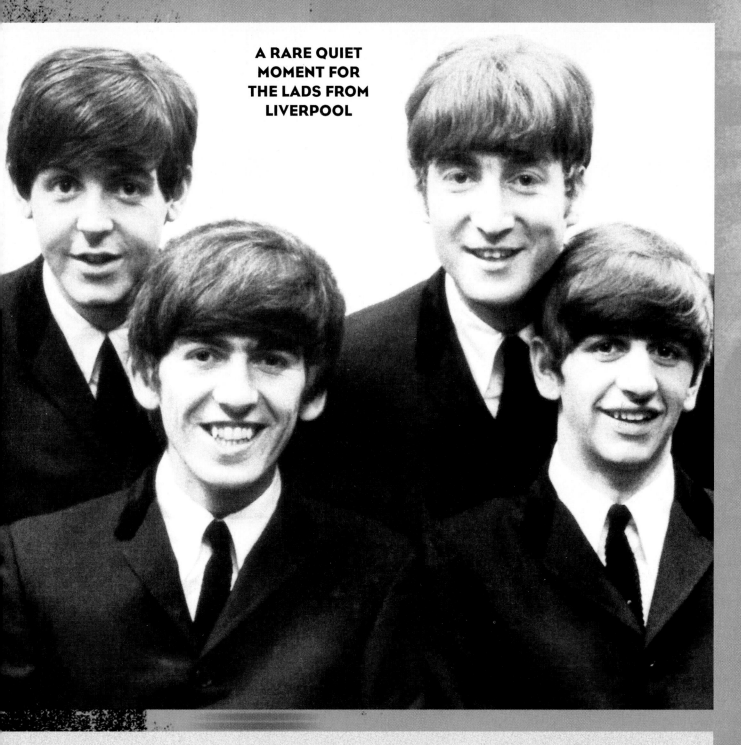

A RARE QUIET
MOMENT FOR
THE LADS FROM
LIVERPOOL

Capitol's "butchery" of their albums in the United States. After protests from retailers, the cover was replaced by a far more placid image of a steamer trunk. Today, copies of the original album jacket are worth thousands of dollars.

## IT'S A RIOT

The Beatles continued to pack stadiums around the world during much of 1966. Performing before uncontrollable, screaming fans was beginning to take a harsh toll on the boys. Appearing in Japan, the group received death threats from militant students who objected to their performance at Budokan. When they snubbed a party in the Philippines hosted by President Ferdinand Marcos, a near riot erupted in Manila.

Anti-Beatle sentiment hit the United States, particularly in the southern states, when Lennon made a characteristically flippant comment to a newspaper reporter saying that The Beatles were "more popular than Jesus." People burned Beatles records in public and the hooded Ku Klux Klan launched a smear campaign ☞

to stamp out the Beatles menace.

Following the release of "Rubber Soul," their most mature effort to date, in August 1966, the exhausted and emotionally spent Beatles embarked on their final U.S. tour, playing their last official performance at San Francisco's Candlestick Park on August 29. The group said they wanted to curb the live performances to concentrate on more extensive studio recordings. But their decreased visibility fueled media speculation that a breakup was possible.

The controversy surrounding the final concerts and possible fractions within the group had no negative impact on the quality of their work. The hit machine continued producing such chart toppers as "Paperback Writer," "Yellow Submarine" and "Eleanor Rigby," along with the album "Revolver."

After 1966, The Beatles worked almost exclusively in recording studios. Their pin-up, "mop top" look was replaced in photographs by the four donning mustaches and Lennon wearing wire-rimmed glasses (his near-sightedness was previously

concealed by contact lenses). The year included such recordings as "Penny Lane" and "Strawberry Fields Forever." This fantastic single is considered by many to be the zenith of the songwriting powers of Lennon and McCartney.

## LANDMARK ALBUM

The Beatles spent much of early 1967 in the studio recording 13 new tracks for their groundbreaking concept album, "Sgt. Pepper's Lonely Hearts Club Band." Not merely an album with stand-alone singles, "Sgt. Pepper's" broke all the rules by intertwining songs (one track actually merged into the next) that captured the cogent aspects of the 1960s youth culture – a culture that included pop art (Andy Warhol), outlandish fashions, drugs, a backlash against parental control and the upheaval and confusion caused by the escalating war in Vietnam. Indeed, to this day, "Sgt. Pepper's Lonely Hearts Club Band" frequently tops polls on what release constitutes the best album of all time.

The album included "Lucy in ☞

the Sky With Diamonds," "When I'm 64" and "Day in the Life." As a final gimmick, the orchestra was recorded beyond a frequency capable of being heard by humans, meaning the final note was audible only to dogs. The album proved that The Beatles had not lost their playfulness.

And the innovation didn't end with the songs. "Sgt. Pepper's" cover art boasted the famous mannequin-based photo collage, which included pictures of every influence on their lives that they could remember. The album also had cardboard cut-out figurines, and for the first time on a pop record, printed lyrics.

While "Sgt. Pepper's" went on to win four Grammys, including best album, The Beatles appeared on a live worldwide television broadcast, singing "All You Need Is Love." The song, which provided a powerful message during the turbulent Vietnam period, shot to No. 1 on record charts throughout the world, keeping Beatlemania alive a while longer.

On August 27, 1967, tragedy befell the group when Beatles manager Brian Epstein was found dead, the

victim of an overdose of the drug Carbitrol. With spiritual guidance from the Maharishi Mahesh Yogi, the group calmly accepted the loss of its manager, opted not to hire a new one and assumed complete control over the group's collective musical career. The Beatles' next project – a BBC special and accompanying concept album "Magical Mystery Tour" – proved to be a misstep. Critically panned, this project is considered by some to represent the beginning of the end of The Beatles.

## AN APPLE FALLS FROM THE TREE

In 1968, The Beatles continued to take greater control of their careers and formed their own corporation and record label, Apple.

"We've already bought all of our dreams," McCartney said at the time regarding incorporation. "We want to share that possibility with others. When we were touring and when the adoration and hysteria were at a peak, if we'd been the shrewd operators we were often made out to be, we might have thought - 'that's nice!'

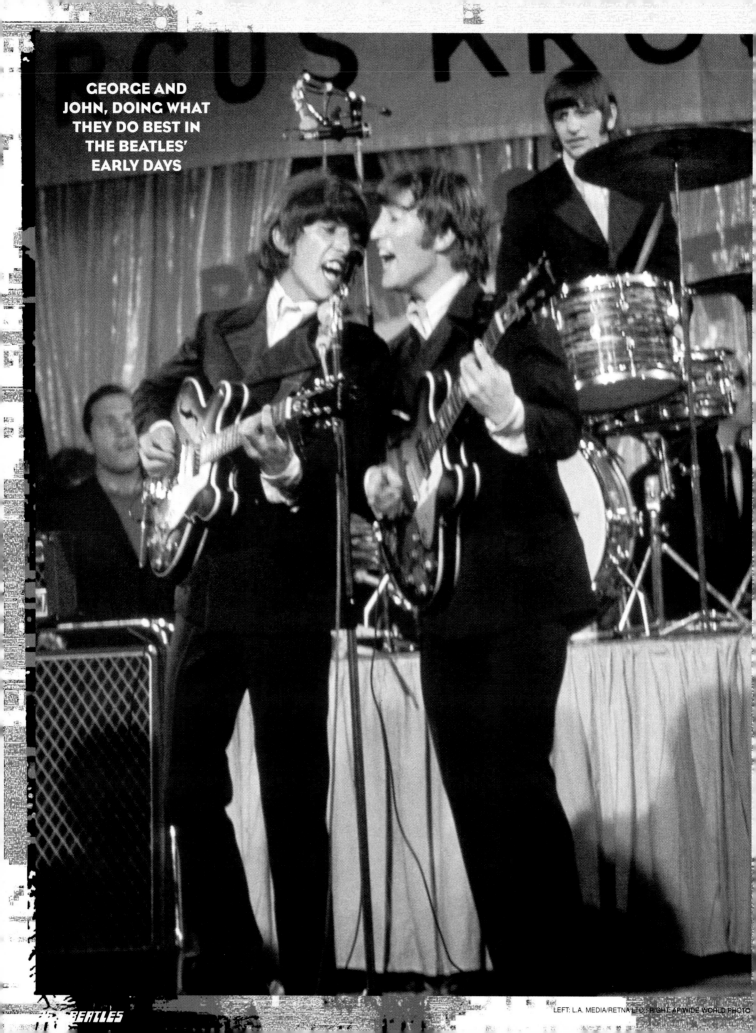

GEORGE AND JOHN, DOING WHAT THEY DO BEST IN THE BEATLES' EARLY DAYS

Ah, click. Let's use this for our own evil ends.' But there was no desire in any of our heads to take over the world. That was Hitler. That's what he wanted to do. There is, however, a desire to get power in order to use it for good."

The boys began recording songs for a new double album, but artistic differences resulted in members of the group storming out of the session, fueling more talk that the group's breakup was imminent.

The result of these sessions is popularly referred to as the "White Album" because the vinyl disc was released with a stark white cover. Officially, however, the LP was called "The Beatles."

The album had glimmers of brilliance, including "Back in the USSR," "Julia" and "Blackbird." The album also featured an appearance by Eric Clapton on guitar on "While My Guitar Gently Weeps." Like the Rolling Stones' "Exile On Main Street," the so-called "White Album" has grown in stature over the years and is more beloved now than when it was first released. ☞

**PAUL IS THE LAST BEATLE TO GIVE IN AND GET A MUSTACHE.**

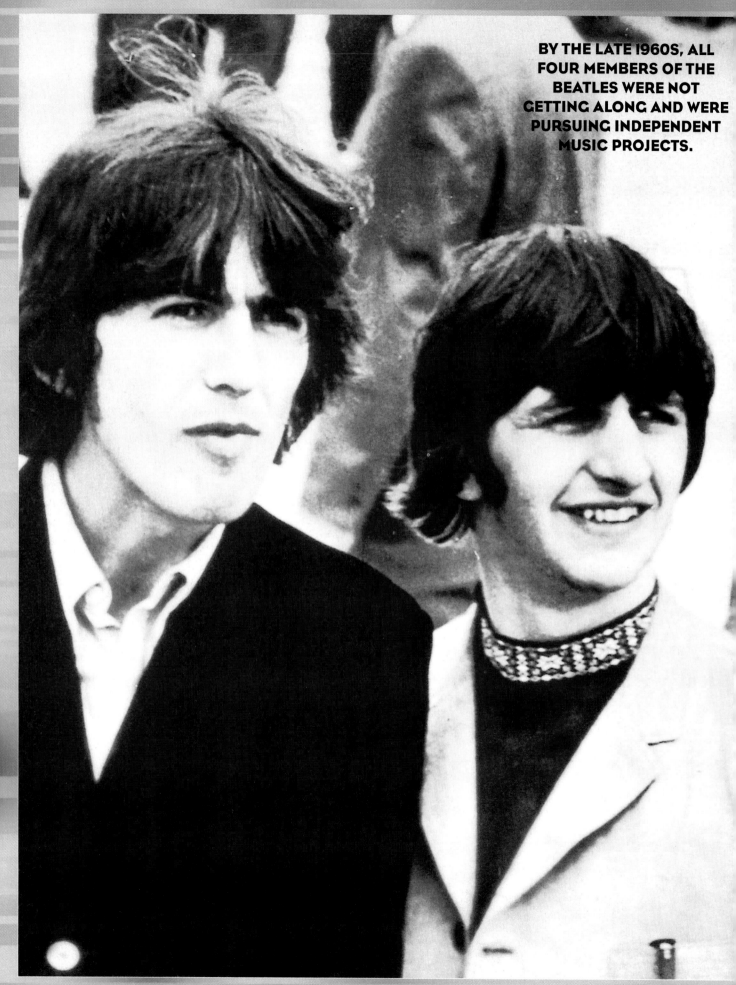

BY THE LATE 1960S, ALL
FOUR MEMBERS OF THE
BEATLES WERE NOT
GETTING ALONG AND WERE
PURSUING INDEPENDENT
MUSIC PROJECTS.

YOKO ONO, JOHN LENNON AND PAUL McCARTNEY ARRIVE FOR THE LONDON PREMIERE OF THE MOVIE 'YELLOW SUBMARINE' IN JULY 1968.

The first Apple single, "Hey Jude," was a cheerful hit that stretched for seven minutes. The Beatles' next film project, "Yellow Submarine," (inspired by the song) was fully animated. Despite the upbeat tone of the film, by late 1968, all of The Beatles were hardly speaking to each other, working mostly on independent music projects.

In a 1968 *Rolling Stone* interview, Lennon described the group's songs as "abstract art."

"It's just that when you have to think about it to write it, it just means that you labored at it. But when you just say it, man, you know you're saying it, it's a continuous flow. The same as when you're recording or just playing. You come out of a thing and

you know 'I've been there,' and it was nothing, it was just pure, and that's what we're looking for all the time, really."

In January 1969, the band returned to the studio to record a live album, without any overdubs. Cameras were present at these last recording sessions, which ran through dozens of songs, many of which they had not ☞

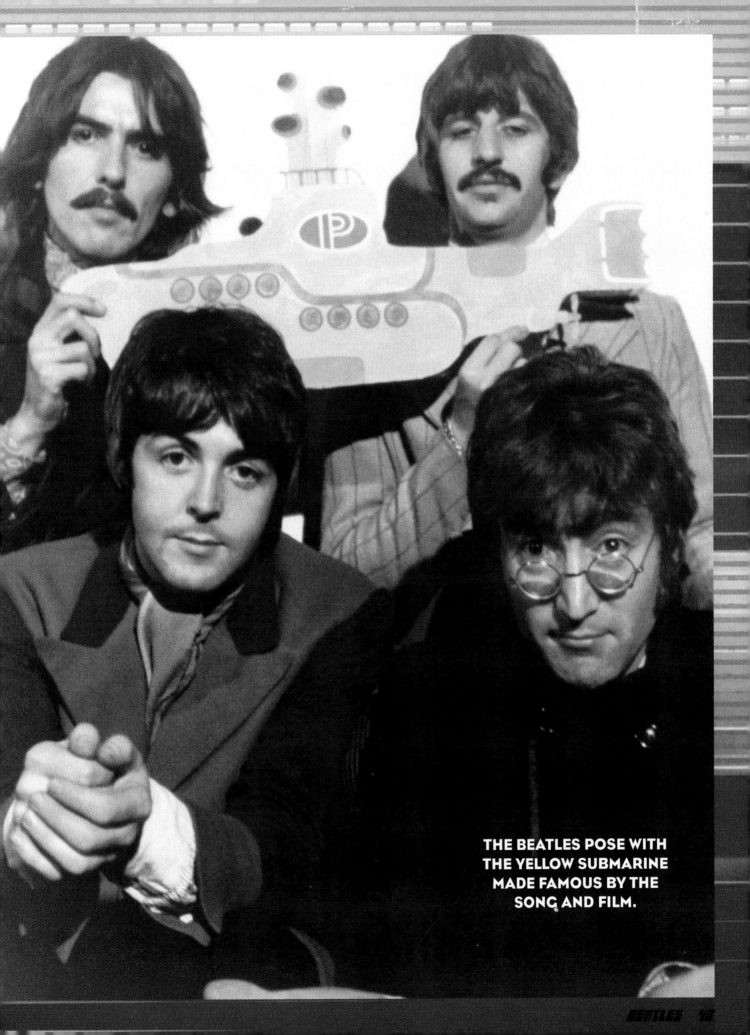

THE BEATLES POSE WITH
THE YELLOW SUBMARINE
MADE FAMOUS BY THE
SONG AND FILM.

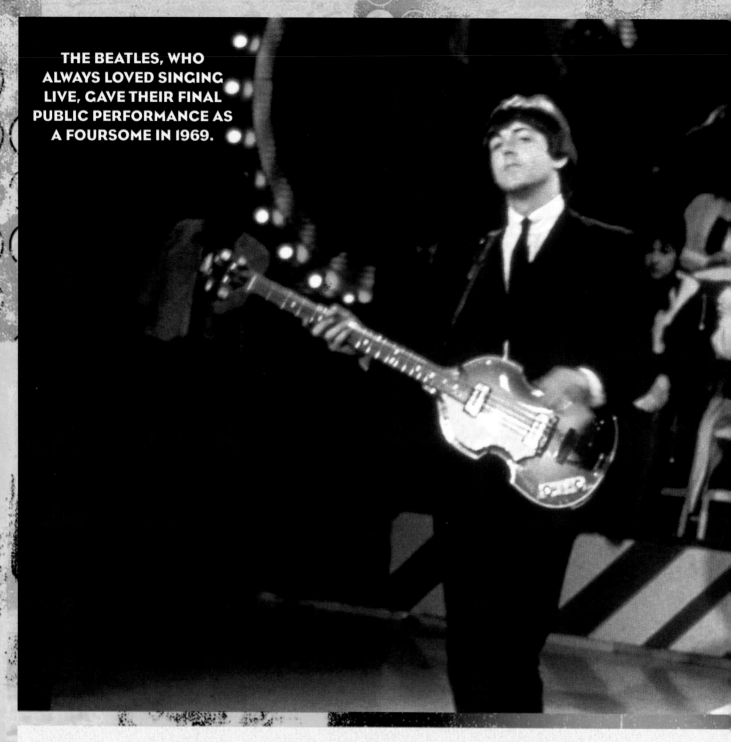

THE BEATLES, WHO ALWAYS LOVED SINGING LIVE, GAVE THEIR FINAL PUBLIC PERFORMANCE AS A FOURSOME IN 1969.

played since their early days in Hamburg. Under the working title "Get Back" (also the name of a hit single), the group, for an accompanying film, performed live in front of a small audience on the rooftop of the Apple studios in London. It was to be their final public performance as a foursome.

While preparing the album, the group continually bickered over creative issues, and the project was shelved amid more hard feelings.

On March 12, 1969, McCartney married American photographer Linda Eastman. That was followed shortly by Lennon's marriage to Yoko Ono.

Attempting to regroup, The Beatles named Allen Klein as their new business manager in May, despite McCartney's objections, who was lobbying for his new father-in-law to serve in that capacity.

In an effort to patch things up or at least present a unified public front, the band reconvened one last time at EMI studios to record "Abbey Road." Despite the continuing conflict, the group produced an artistically cohesive work. The accompanying

single coupled Lennon's "Come Together" (an apt title) with Harrison's haunting "Something." Harrison received due recognition and the song went on to become the group's second biggest popular hit behind "Yesterday."

## TROUBLED WATERS

With various solo projects in the works, the four Beatles stumbled into the '70s, steadfastly denying rumors of a band breakup. As early as September 1969, Lennon told his bandmates that he wanted to split, but renegotiations with EMI put a temporary halt to that talk.

The internal turmoil was stoked when Allen Klein brought in producer Phil Spector to produce and overdub of the album "Get Back" (released in May 1970 as "Let It Be"). The album did not chart any new musical ground for the group, but did contain The Beatles' final No. 1 hit, "Long and Winding Road."

The album's debut was preceded by the release of the dreary film *Let It Be*.

During this time it was McCartney who was embroiled in the most ☞

JOHN LENNON AND YOKO ONO OUTSIDE THEIR HOME IN ENGLAND IN 1972

controversy with his mates. In order to avoid hurting sales of "Let it Be," Paul was encouraged to delay the release of "McCartney," his solo album. In protest, the stubborn McCartney released his album in April, one month before "Let it Be," and publicly said he was quitting the band. On December 31, 1970, McCartney sued Klein to break up the group.

This didn't go over well with the other three members, who wanted to pursue solo careers while at the same time retain the flexibility to regroup periodically for selected projects. Any chance of a reunion seemed hopeless, and Apple was mired in a financial and legal mess.

"The whole Beatle thing – it's like

it was all years ago – like going back a distance more than anything," said McCartney in a 1971 *Life* magazine interview. "And that's the whole point. The Beatles are really finished, over with, and it's just each of us alone now, living our lives the way we choose."

During the 1970s each member of The Beatles did indeed go their

separate ways and release solo albums with mixed degrees of success. McCartney, performing with his wife, Linda, in the group Wings, was the most successful. Lennon recorded periodically with his wife Yoko and continued to be a high-profile voice for radical politics. In 1975, he took an extended hiatus to spend time with his newborn son, Sean.

Rumors surfaced during the 1970s about a possible reunion, but nothing ever happened. In a publicity stunt, *Saturday Night Live* producer Lorne Michaels offered The Beatles $3,000 to perform on the show.

The closest the lads came to any reunion was in 1973 when each member contributed to a Ringo Starr song, "I'm the Greatest."

## THE DAY THE MUSIC DIED

All chances of The Beatles ever reuniting came to an abrupt and tragic end on December 8, 1980, when a deranged fan, Mark David Chapman, gunned down John Lennon outside his New York City apartment. As with the assassinations of President ☞

John F. Kennedy and civil rights leader Martin Luther King, many people recall what they were doing when they first heard of Lennon's murder. All-night vigils were held outside Lennon's apartment as thousands of fans came to pay tribute, many leaving flowers and candles on a sidewalk.

Although The Beatles' last album was released in 1970, demand for their recordings remains high, with Capitol continuing to reap large profits. Publishing rights to all Lennon and McCartney songs were sold in the '80s for hundreds of millions of dollars; at one point they were the property of Michael Jackson. Although Capitol issued such singles and out-takes compilations as "Past Masters" and "Rarities," much of The Beatles' unreleased material was already being sold in the form of illegal bootlegs.

By the 1990s, the surviving Beatles along with Yoko Ono settled their contractual disputes, allowing for the re-release of long unavailable recordings. They also collaborated on a 1995 documentary of the group. ☞

PUBLISHING RIGHTS TO SONGS BY PAUL McCARTNEY AND JOHN LENNON SOLD FOR HUNDREDS OF MILLIONS OF DOLLARS IN THE 1980S.

**JOHN AND YOKO IN THE POST-BEATLES YEARS**

The trio laid down music for two Lennon demo out-takes, "Free as a Bird" and "Real Love."

The following year, America proved that Beatlemania was far from dead. The three double-album releases – "Beatles Anthology" 1, 2 and 3 – sold more than 15 million copies in less than a year. Not only did it introduce a whole new generation to Beatles music, but Paul, George and Ringo took home three Grammys for the project.

Sadly, the dissolution of The Beatles under less-than-positive circumstances was a disappointing ending for the group that had a huge impact on music in the 20th century. Some 30 years later, the quality of the songs, both musically and lyrically, has not diminished.

Now, the new official publication, "The Beatles Anthology," offers fans a rare, up-close look at the boys from Liverpool who became pop music icons. The book contains 340,000 words and more than 1,300 images, including previously unseen shots.

It's another step that proves that the beat goes on for The Beatles. ∎

MUSIC BY JOHN LENNON AND THE REST OF THE BEATLES STILL ENDURES MORE THAN 30 YEARS LATER.

# RINGO STARR

BY DAVID FANTLE AND THOMAS JOHNSON

Ringo Starr was born on July 7, 1940, in Liverpool, England. Named after his father, he was the only child of Richard Starkey and Elsie Gleave. The family resided in a six-room terrace house in a poor and rough working-class section of Liverpool known as the Dingle. Richard Sr. left home when little Richard, now called Ritchie, was only 3 years old.

In 1944, Ritchie and his mother moved to a smaller, less expensive terrace house around the corner. Ritchie called 10 Admiral Grove home until he moved to London with The Beatles. Determined to support herself and her child, Elsie went to work as a barmaid, often leaving Ritchie in the care of neighbors or his paternal grandparents.

According to the Ringo Starr Homepage, at the age of 5, Ritchie started school at St. Silas Infants School, but his academic career hit the first of many snags when, at age 6, he developed appendicitis. His appendix ruptured, resulting in peritonitis and a

BEATLES 53

10-week coma. Elsie was told on several occasions that her boy would not live, but eventually, to the doctor's surprise, he came around and his condition slowly improved.

Ritchie never cared much for school, and the fact that he was so far behind didn't help. He would often play truant, a fact that no doubt influenced his dismal showing on the Review examination. Since he didn't pass Review, he ended up attending Dinglevale Secondary Modern School at age 11.

In 1953, with Ritchie's enthusiastic blessing, Elsie married Harry Graves. That same year Ritchie developed pleurisy. Complications resulted in another hospitalization that lasted two years. Despite all these hardships, Ritchie, by all accounts, remained a contented, easy-going individual — if somewhat quiet and thoughtful. When he emerged from the hospital at 15, he knew that returning to school was out of the question. He had simply missed too much and felt that he could never catch up.

After several menial jobs (messenger boy, barman and apprentice joiner) Ritchie, now 17, took advantage of the skiffle craze that had just taken England by storm. Along with two friends, he started the Eddie Clayton skiffle group and served as percussionist. The strictly amateur group played parties and local competitions. In December 1957, Harry Graves bought his stepson his first real set of drums — a second-hand set that cost 10 pounds.

In March 1959, Ritchie joined a bona fide band called The Hurricanes. It was then (taking a cue from his penchant for wearing flashy rings on his fingers) that Ritchie Starkey became Ringo Starr. His big numbers during this time included "You're Sixteen," "Big Noise From Winnetka" and "Alley Oop."

By the fall of 1960, The Hurricanes were topping the bill at the Kaiserskeller in Hamburg,

Germany. It was there that Ringo made the acquaintance of another Liverpool-based band, The Beatles. Ringo got on well with all the members of The Beatles — most notably with George Harrison.

In 1962, after giving up on a dream to migrate to Texas for a factory job in Houston, Ringo quit The Hurricanes and took The Beatles up on their offer of a job as the group's new drummer (replacing Pete Best).

Ringo served The Beatles well. As a drummer, he never tried to over-shadow the music, working always with the song and the singer. On stage he seemed content to stay in the background, feeding the others with his steady backbeat. Despite his rather sad-looking hound-dog expression, Ringo was a happy and sensitive individual. In interviews and in The Beatles' movies, his natural wit and wry humor emerged. He could be as funny as John, but without the biting sarcasm. People were drawn to him because of his friendly easy-going manner. He became known to the world as "The Lovable Beatle."

"Ringo is Ringo, that's all there is to it," said John Lennon. "And he's every bloody bit as warm, unassuming, funny and kind as he seems. He was quite simply the heart of The Beatles."

Indeed, after the group split up, it seemed for a long while that Ringo was the only one who stayed on good terms with the other three.

On February 11, 1965, Ringo married his Liverpool sweetheart, Mary (Maureen) Cox. They had met back in his Hamburg days when she had been a student hairdresser. Together they had two boys (Zak and Jason) and a daughter (Lee) before Ringo and Mary divorced in 1975.

When The Beatles officially split up in December 1970, Ringo already had two solo albums behind him, "Sentimental Journey" and "Beaucoups of Blues." Ringo had also drummed on Lennon's "Plastic Ono Band and George Harrison's three-volume "All Things Must Pass." He also acted in the movies *Candy* and *The Magic Christian*. The next year he released "It Don't Come Easy," the first of what would be a string of hit singles including "Back Off Boogaloo."

In February 1980, Ringo appeared in the movie *Caveman*. It was while filming in Mexico that he met and fell in love with costar Barbara Bach, an American model and actress best known for her part in the James Bond movie, *The Spy Who Loved Me*. Throughout the '80s the peripatetic Ringo gigged, recorded and starred in a clutch of movies. But the latter part of the decade was a rather quiet time for the lad from Liverpool due to his increasingly heavy dependence on alcohol. Perhaps the most fulfilling event of 1985 was the birth of his first, and as yet only, grandchild, Tatia Jayne, the daughter of Zak and his wife Sarah.

Other highlights of Ringo's post-Beatle career include a stint acting as Mr. Conductor on TV's Shining Time Station children's series; the opening of his restaurant, The Brassier, in Atlanta, Georgia; appearances in commercials for Sun Country Classic Wine Coolers; and The Beatles' induction into the Rock and Roll Hall of Fame in 1988.

In 1989, a sober and revitalized Ringo embarked on his first-ever solo concert tour with his All-Starr Band, which released a couple of albums. In recent years, Ringo has appeared with his two surviving Beatles bandmates in various concert settings — many of them to benefit charitable causes.

Today, Ringo and Barbara call Monte Carlo home, but they maintain houses in Los Angeles and Colorado.

"Ringo's just a lad," said Paul McCartney. "Everybody always loved him … He's just a lovable, interesting and intelligent bloke." ∎

RINGO STARR

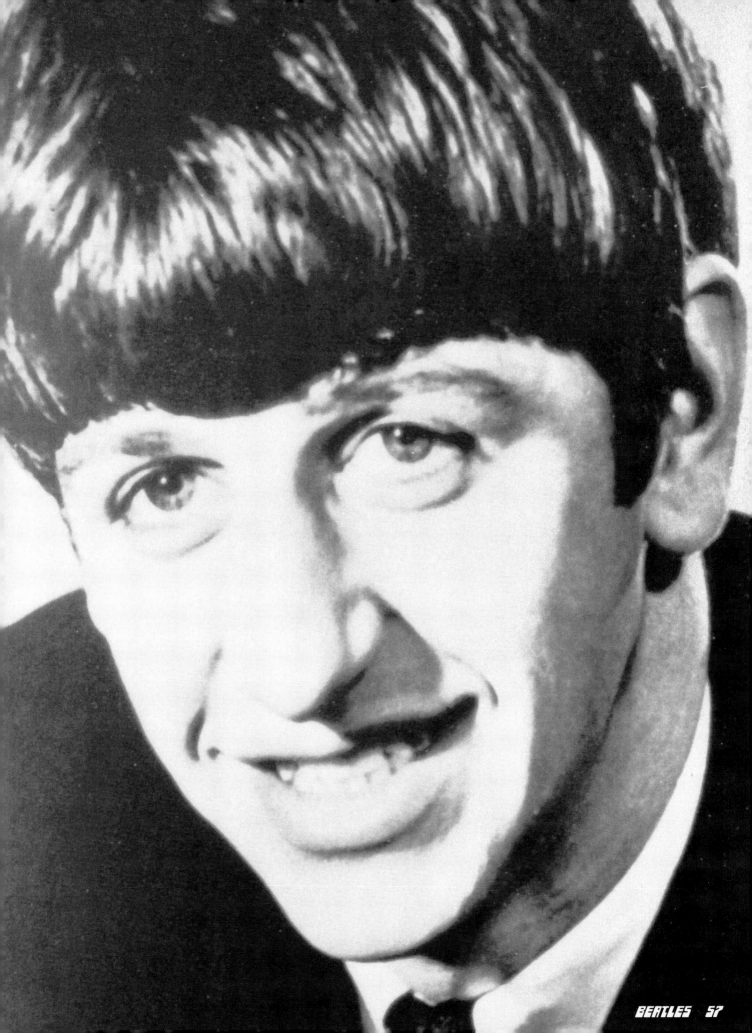

BEATLES 57

# RINGO STARR

# RINGO STARR

# GEORGE HARRISON

BY DAVID FANTLE AND THOMAS JOHNSON

George Harrison was born on February 25, 1943, in the midst of World War II rationing and purging. His mother was Louise Harrison, a grocer, and his father, Harry Harrison, was a sailor. George is the youngest of four children and was a very bright and well-behaved child who was eager to learn. The Harrisons lived in the working class section of Liverpool in Arnold Grove. He attended Dovedale Primary School, where John Lennon was already three years ahead of him. In 1949, when George was 6, the Harrisons moved to Speke, England.

George's musical career began at age 13, when his mother bought him his first guitar — a three-pound acoustic from a friend of George's father. George was a quick study and began to imitate the sounds on the pop records he heard. While he was still attending the Liverpool Institute in 1955, George met Paul McCartney. George first saw John Lennon when he was playing with his band, The ☛

BEATLES 63

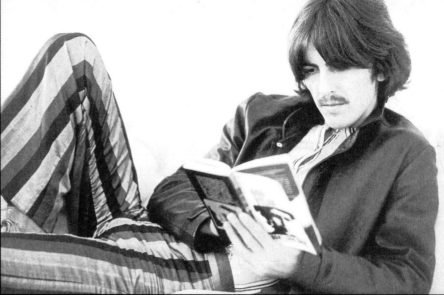

Quarrymen, at a church gathering. It wasn't George but Paul who first joined The Quarrymen, but George was later accepted into the group when he played the tune "Raunchy" perfectly.

After a couple of name changes (and band member changes) in the summer of 1960, The Beatles were hired by Bruno Koschmider to play at the Indra in Hamburg, Germany. They crossed the English Channel and played in the seedy Kaiserkeller. It was here that The Beatles developed their signature style and formed themselves into a tight-knit group. But the German police soon found out that George was 17, a year too young to be working in Hamburg. The Beatles and George were promptly deported back to England.

In Liverpool, the group became famous in its own right. The guys played the Cavern Club, and opportunity knocked one day during a lunchtime session when Brian Epstein (a local record shop owner) stopped into the club, liked what he heard and became their manager.

Signing on to Parlophone Records in London, Sir George Martin became the group's producer. Success came quickly. The Beatles were the driving force in pop music for years to come. They were the first British rock 'n' roll band to make it big in America, and they paved the way for many other bands.

Upon arriving stateside, folk-rock poet, Bob Dylan introduced the band to marijuana — the drug would influence

The Beatles' style (especially George) from that day forward.

With worldwide success eminent, another big event occurred for George. On the set of The Beatles' first movie, *A Hard Day's Night*, he met his first wife, Patricia Anne Boyd. Patti was a swinging '60s model; her dolly bird makeup and sweet sex-kittenish attitude bewitched George. They were married on January 21, 1966, with fellow band member Paul McCartney in attendance.

In 1965, George first heard the sitar, played by an Indian musician on the set of The Beatles' second movie, *Help!* George bought one and started to play. George on sitar first appeared in the song "Norwegian Wood," and it sparked a craze for the twangy sound. Soon, the Rolling Stones were using the instrument on "Paint It Black."

Meeting Ravi Shankar, an accomplished sitar virtuoso, at Peter Sellers' house was a happy coincidence, too. Ravi had heard George's pop hindi tune, "Love You Too" from The Beatles' "Rubber Soul" album, and Harrison asked Shankar to teach him the sitar. They became close friends for years to come. George and the other Beatles soon became interested in all things Indian. For his part, George fell into the Transcendental Meditation movement head first. The other Beatles followed, and soon they became embroiled in the hoax of the decade, the Maharishi Mahesh Yogi.

During this time period sprung Harrison's psychedelica. He had become better at composing for the sitar and produced some lovely ballads, including "Within You, Without You" and "Inner Light." Most were based on Indian spiritual passages George had received. Taking more and more drugs fueled his spiritual insight and he was visibly stoned in the The Beatles' third movie, *Magical Mystery Tour*.

Obvious, public displays of drug use and being high resulted in George and Patti's bungalow being raided in 1969. George was subsequently arrested for possession of an illegal substance (hashish) and both were immediately released on bail. George later became disillusioned with drugs after seeing the Haight-Ashbury district, describing it as nightmarish.

George next took up with the cultish

married Eric Clapton) when George was planning "The Concert for Bangladesh." Enlisting the help of such friends as Bob Dylan, Ringo Starr, Eric Clapton and Ravi Shankar, the benefit concert was a huge success.

In 1974, George met Olivia Arias (a 27-year-old secretary for A&M Records) at a party. It was love at first sight — for both of them. They both shared deep religious convictions (at the time, George was a steadfast Hindu). Over the next year, they became closer with Olivia finally moving in to George's estate, Friar Park. In 1978, George became a father when Olivia gave birth to his only child, Dhani. They were also married that same year.

In 1980, George published his autobiography, *I, Me, Mine*. Reportedly, John Lennon was angry because George didn't mention him anywhere in the book. Only a few short months later, John was felled by an assassin's bullet. This prompted George to write a tribute song to John, "All Those Years Ago." The song was a hit and sold well, but George and become increasingly jaded with the music industry since its turn to New Wave.

Back in 1978, George started a movie company, Handmade Films, to fund a Monty Python film, *The Life of Brian*. His company helped to revitalize the British film industry by producing such hits as *Time Bandits*, *Mona Lisa* and *Shanghai Surprise* starring Sean Penn and his then-wife, Madonna.

George heralded his return to the recording industry with his smash hit "I Got My Mind Set On You." Happy to be performing again, George next teamed up with Bob Dylan, Roy Orbison, Tom Petty and Jeff Lynne as The Traveling Wilburys. Their titular album was a huge success.

After a couple more albums (and the death of Orbison), the group amicably disbanded. George next toured in Japan accompanied by his old friend – "husband in law" – Eric Clapton. After working with Paul McCartney on new material for ABC TV's *Beatles Anthology*, George was diagnosed with throat cancer. Fortunately, the tumor was caught early and he has completely recovered.

Another scare occurred last year when George was stabbed inside his own home by an obsessed Beatles fan. George's lung was punctured, but again, he made a full recovery. ∎

Hare Krishna movement that was to drive a stake between him and his wife and nudge her into the arms of his friend and fellow rocker Eric Clapton. After the messy dissolution of Apple Corps, a joint venture with his three Beatles bandmates, the group finally split in 1970. Finally off The Beatles merry-go-round, George was at last free to compose his own music.

The '70s tested George's ability as a solo artist. He started off the decade by compiling all the songs he wrote that Paul and John had rejected during his Beatles days and put them into a three-record album, "All Things Must Pass." The album was a smash and his song, "My Sweet Lord," stayed at the No. 1 spot on the Billboard chart for four weeks. To this day, critics consider the album George's best solo effort.

Despite career success, George and Patti's marriage was disintegrating. The unhappy couple split up in 1972 (they divorced in 1977 whereupon Patti

GEORGE HARRISON

BEATLES 67

GEORGE HARRISON

GEORGE HARRISON

# JOHN LENNON

BY DAVID FANTLE AND THOMAS JOHNSON

John Winston Lennon was born on October 9, 1940, in England's northern industrial seaport of Liverpool, the son of a porter father who deserted the family when John was 3. When his father resurfaced once John reached stardom, John slammed the door in his face. He later recalled, "I don't feel as if I owe him anything. He never helped me. I got there by myself."

Considered the most intellectual and outspoken member of The Beatles, John was influenced early on by legendary American rockers such as Chuck Berry, Jerry Lee Lewis, Little Richard and especially Elvis Presley.

John attended secondary school in Liverpool, then went on to Liverpool College of Art, where he married a classmate, Cynthia Powell. They later divorced, and in 1969, John married Yoko Ono, a Japanese-American artist who was pregnant ☞

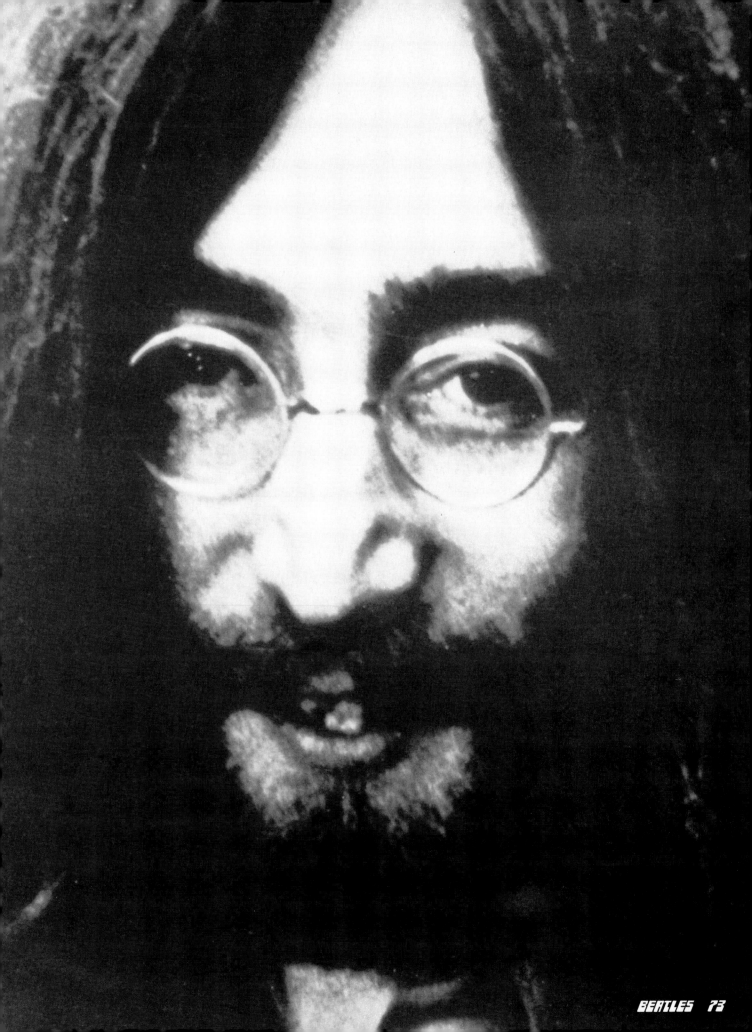

BEATLES 73

with his second child at the time. John later said of the untraditional courtship, 'We went to Paris on our honeymoon, then interrupted our honeymoon to get married on the Rock of Gibraltar."

The seed for The Beatles band dates back to 1955, when Lennon met Paul McCartney at a Liverpool, England church social. The two started performing as a duo, called The Quarrymen, and were joined three years later by George Harrison. Ringo Starr didn't come into the band until 1962 — a year before The Beatles hit the top of the charts in Britain with "Please Please Me."

In 1958, John's mother, Julia, was hit by a car and killed at the age of 44. The traumatic accident would profoundly affect Lennon for the rest of his life. The year 1960 was pivotal for the Fab Four and marks several big changes for the group. After trying on several different names for size, the group finally decided on The Beatles. And in January, Stu Sutcliffe, a friend of John's from school, joined the band as bass player (even though he didn't know how to play the instrument).

After formally making record shop owner Brian Epstein their manager in 1962, things really started to pick up for the group. Epstein transformed The Beatles from a scruffy band with leather pants and jackets to a slickly dressed foursome with suits, ties and mop-top haircuts. John later said that was the

moment that The Beatles "sold out." Also that year, John married Cynthia Powell, who was pregnant with their child (John Charles Julian Lennon). They divorced in 1968.

"Beatlemania" didn't cross the ocean to the United States until 1964, when "I Want to Hold Your Hand" was released and Ed Sullivan invited the foursome to appear on his weekly TV show. "Meet The Beatles" became the best-selling record album in history to that date. That year the British invasion began, and in August 1964, a Beatles film, *A Hard Day's Night,* opened to extraordinary critical and popular acclaim.

But not everything was rosy for The Beatles. In a 1966 interview, John said, "Christianity will go. It will vanish and shrink. I needn't argue with that; I'm right and will be proved right." He added, "Right now, The Beatles are more popular than Jesus Christ." The statements caused an anti-Beatles backlash with boycotts, record burnings and threats. John issued a formal apology at a press conference.

Beatles albums to follow "Meet The Beatles" included "Rubber Soul," "Revolver," "Sgt. Pepper's Lonely Heart's Club Band," "The Beatles (white album)" and "Abbey Road." During their collaboration, the group sold more than 250 million records. But the collaboration ended abruptly in 1970 amid talk of a falling out between John and Paul, in addition to recriminations against the management of their recording company. Some critics blame John's 1969 marriage to Yoko Ono for the breakup of The Beatles — especially after she was denied the "fifth Beatle" status. But John denied it, saying he wanted to leave the group as early as 1966 "but just didn't have the guts."

After The Beatles broke up in 1970, Lennon continued writing songs and recording. But in 1975 he dropped out for five years to "bake bread" and raise his son Sean Taro Ono Lennon (born in 1975). In the post-Beatles years, John released 12 solo albums, including "Unfinished Music No. 1: Two Virgins" and the "John Lennon Plastic Ono Band." Perhaps the most stirring song he wrote during that time period is the wistful ballad "Imagine." It quickly

became an anthem for peace.

In 1980, John released his first studio album in five years, "Double Fantasy." It was his last. On December 8 of that year he was gunned down by Mark David Chapman outside of the Dakota Apartments, his home in New York City. In 1994, John Lennon was inducted into the Rock and Roll Hall of Fame.

In summing up John's contribution to music, the entire measure of the man must be taken, including the amazing symbiosis that occurred when he and Paul McCartney collaborated. The Beatles came out of the lower middle class in Liverpool, England during a period of social confrontation among England's youth. The times produced warring cliques of Mods, foppish intellectual sorts, leather-clad bikers … and rock 'n' rollers. When asked to which group The Beatles belonged, John replied, "Neither, we're mockers." It was a telling statement.

John's songs – such as "I Am Lawless," "A Day in the Life" and "Strawberry Fields Forever" – were the wanderings of a restless spirit through existential, uninviting worlds. They told of depression, angst and bizarre discovery. Indeed, John played the crazy jester to the pop sensibility of Paul, whose songs were often slick and frothy. But when the two worked together, legendary music was made. Imagine that. ■

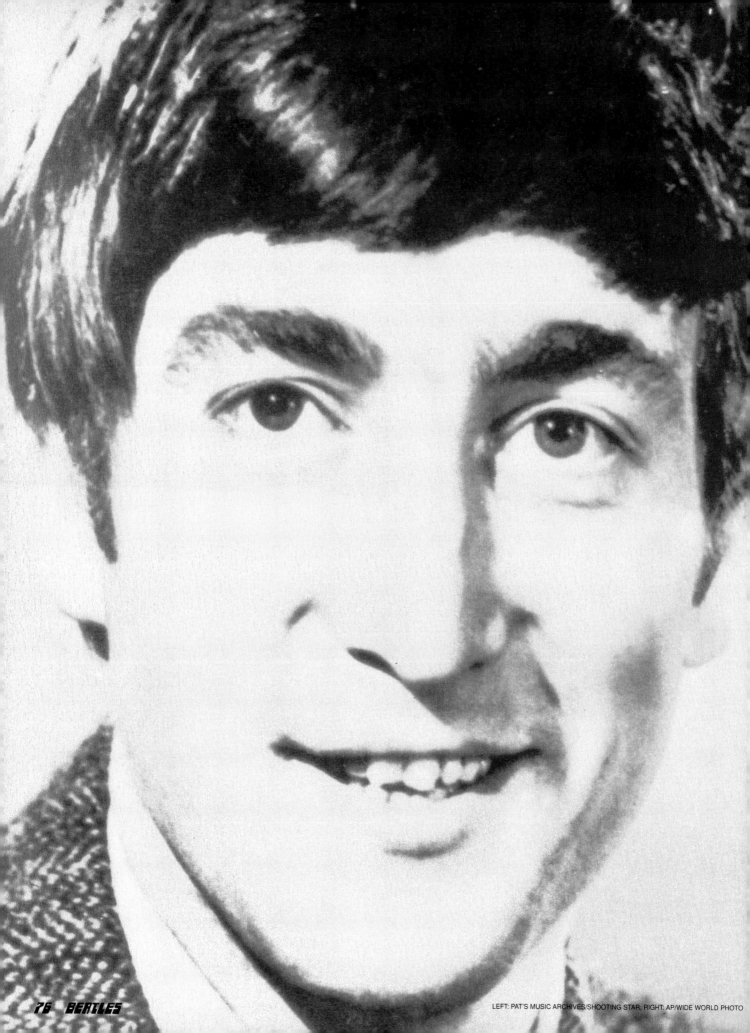

JOHN LENNON

JOHN
LENNON

BEATLES 79

JOHN LENNON

# PAUL McCARTNEY

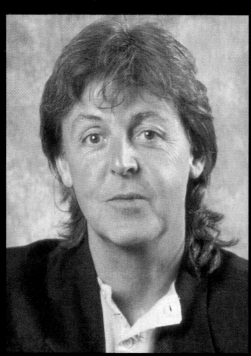

BY DAVID FANTLE AND THOMAS JOHNSON

James Paul McCartney was born in Liverpool, England on June 18, 1942, to working-class parents Jim and Mary. Paul's idyllic childhood was shattered when his mother died from breast cancer. In the wake of her death, Paul asked his father to buy him a guitar. He did, and a legend was born.

Paul attended the Liverpool Institute (where he met George Harrison in 1955). Since writing his first song at the age of 14, Paul has dreamed and dared to be different. In the '60s, as the writer and co-author of The Beatles' greatest songs, he changed the world of music. Also in the '60s – 1967 to be exact – Paul met the love of his life, Linda Eastman, a magazine photojournalist who specialized in covering the rock 'n' roll scene. On March 12, 1969, they married. (They would ultimately have four children together: James, Mary, Heather and Stella).

Coinciding with the breakup of ☞

The Beatles, Paul, in 1971, formed his MPL group of companies and released his debut solo album, "McCartney." Also that year, Paul released his second album "Ram" and the No. 1 single "Another Day." He also formed the group Wings, which released its debut album, "Wild Life," late in the year. In 1973, Wings scored its biggest hit with massively successful "Band On the Run" album (it won two Grammy Awards). Also in 1973, Paul penned the theme song for a James Bond film, *Live and Let Die*.

Through the following three decades, first with his group Wings (which broke up in 1981), and then as a solo artist, Paul continued to break boundaries and to influence the sound of music around the globe.

Indeed, Paul was so prolific and popular in the post-Beatle years that it became a standard joke amongst the younger generation to query, "You mean that Paul McCartney was in a band

before Wings?" Also grist for the humor mill was Paul's incredible wealth; his legal ownership of thousands of songs (including such state anthems as "On Wisconsin"); and the strict vegetarian edicts of his beloved wife and business partner, Linda.

In the 1980s, Paul performed hit duets with Stevie Wonder and Michael Jackson ("Ebony and Ivory" and "The Girl is Mine," respectively). He also starred in the major motion picture, *Give My Regards to Broad Street* with his wife Linda and fellow Beatles alum Ringo Starr and Ringo's wife Barbara Bach.

Paul's boundless talent isn't confined just to rock 'n' roll. In 1990, he was commissioned by the Royal Liverpool Philharmonic Society to write the Liverpool Oratio, which has received more than 100 performances in 20 countries since its premiere in 1991. The double-CD album topped the charts in both the UK and USA and was released on laser disc.

In 1995 – the 30th anniversary of his most acclaimed song "Yesterday" – his second classical work, "A Leaf" premiered at St. James' Palace in the presence of the Prince of Wales. Since then, Paul has taken other steps into the classical form, composing "Stately Horn," "Inebriation," "Spiral" and his major challenge, "Standing Stone."

The previous year, Paul had posthumously inducted John Lennon into the Rock and Roll Hall of Fame. He also reunited with George Harrison and Ringo Starr to record the first new Beatles song in 25 years, "Free As a Bird," completing an unfinished demo tape of John's from 1977. The three former Beatles also recorded another song from an unfinished Lennon demo, "Real Love."

Paul McCartney became Sir Paul McCartney MBE in an investiture ceremony at Buckingham Palace in 1997. And his new album, "Flaming Pie," with hit singles "The World Tonight" and "Young Boy," became a huge worldwide hit (it would become Paul's 81st gold disc, a feat that broke his own world record). And just to remind people that the spirit of the '60s was still alive and well, Paul becomes embroiled in controversy when he revealed his belief that marijuana should be decriminalized (30 years after first signing a petition calling for the legalization of cannabis).

Tragedy struck on April 17, 1998, when Paul's wife Linda succumbed to breast cancer at the age of 56, after having been diagnosed with the disease in 1995. A bereft Paul said, "I have been privileged to been her lover for 30 years, and in all that time, except for one enforced absence, we never spent a single night apart. When people asked why, we would say – "What for?""

Paul has soldiered on during the past couple of years since Linda's death. His latest album, "A Garland for Linda," is a commemoration of their life together, with profits from sales of the album going to fund cancer research. ■

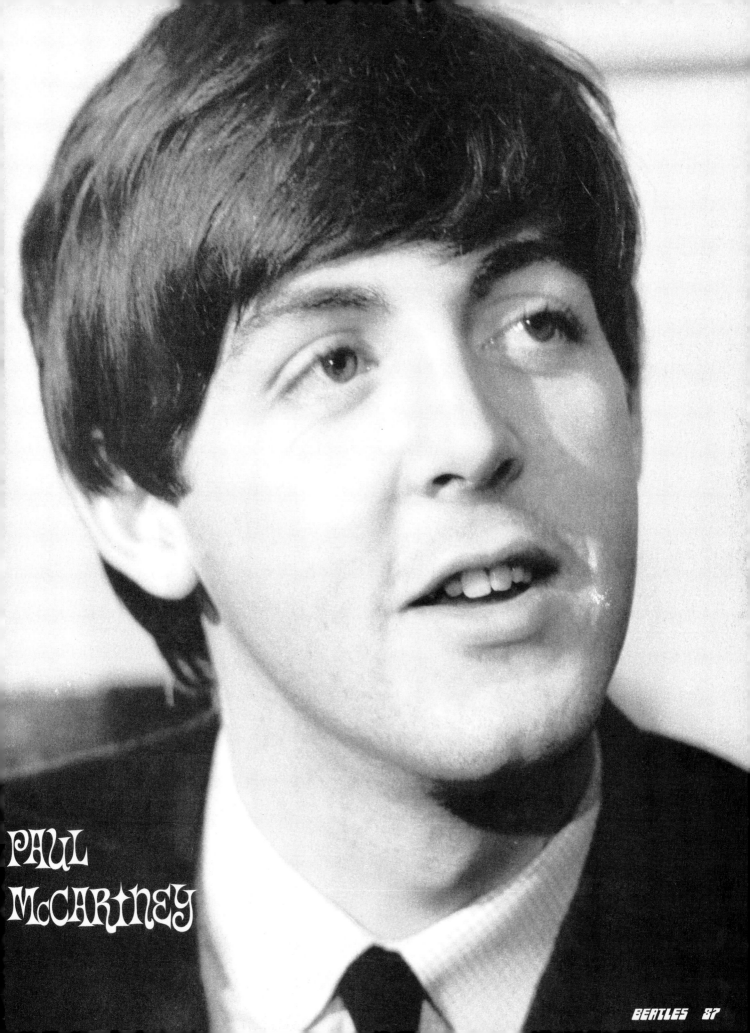

PAUL McCARTNEY

BEATLES 87

PAUL McCARTNEY

BEATLES 89

PAUL McCARTNEY

YAMAHA

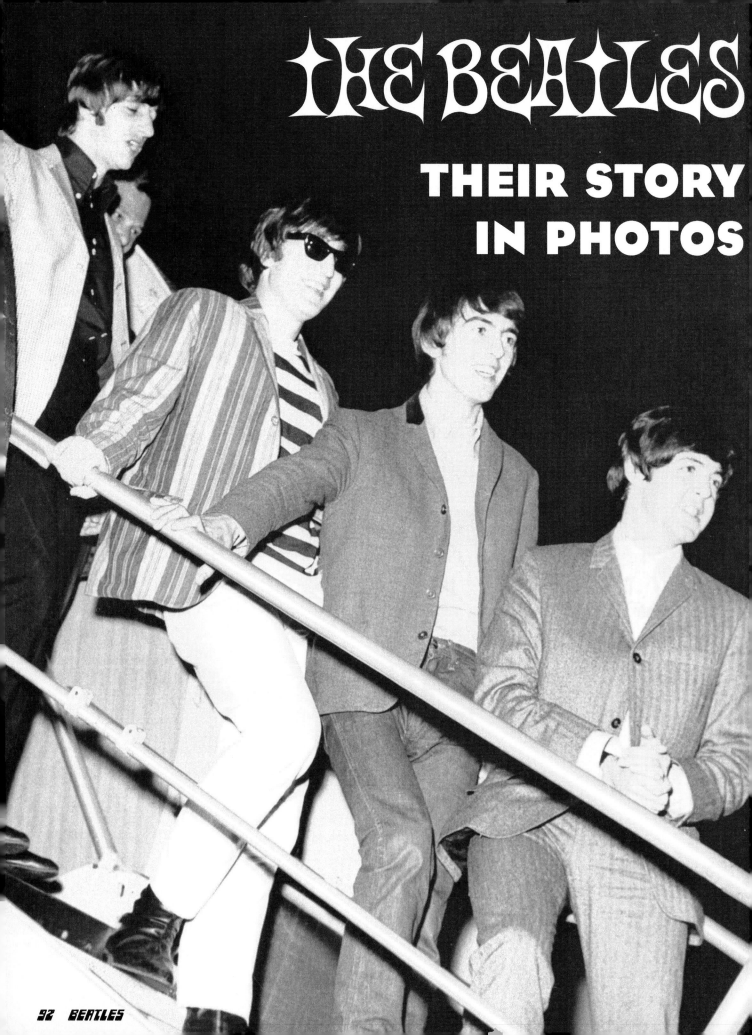

# THE BEATLES

## THEIR STORY IN PHOTOS

LEFT: THE BEATLES DEPLANE IN A VISIT TO LAS VEGAS.

THIS PAGE: THE BEATLES HANG OUT WITH HEAVYWEIGHT BOXER CASSIUS CLAY (LATER KNOWN AS MUHAMMAD ALI) AT CLAY'S MIAMI TRAINING CAMP IN FEBRUARY 1964.

**THE BEATLES POSED FOR THIS PHOTO JUST BEFORE THEY PERFORMED ON 'THE ED SULLIVAN SHOW' IN 1964.**

MUSICIANS GEORGE HARRISON AND PAUL SIMON PERFORM TOGETHER IN 1979.

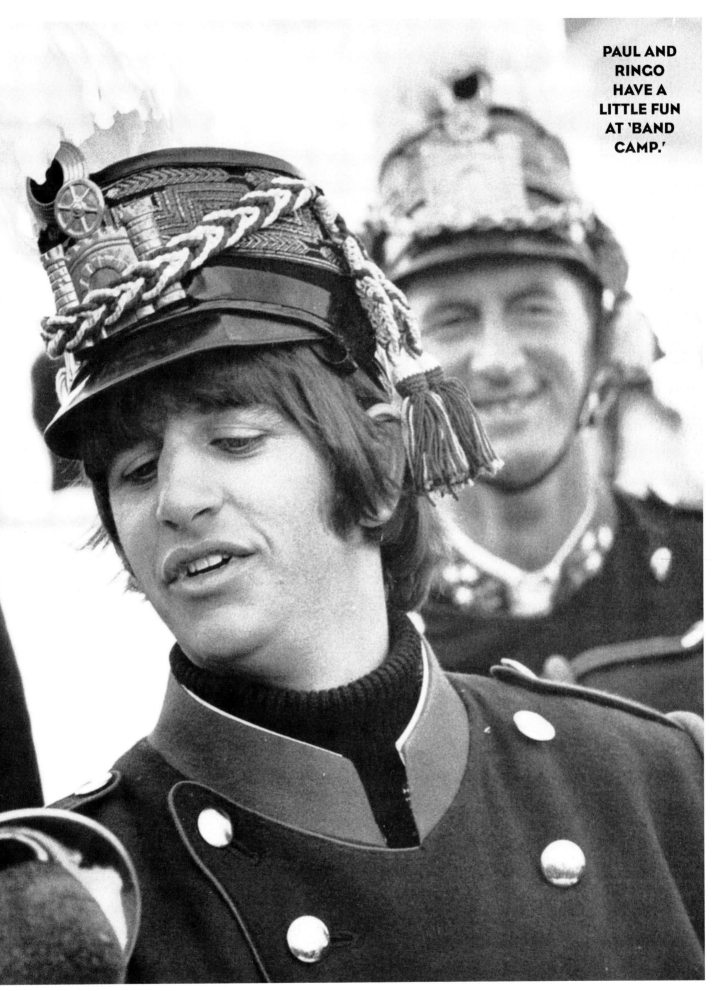

PAUL AND RINGO HAVE A LITTLE FUN AT 'BAND CAMP.'

RINGO STARR AND JOHN LENNON ADDRESS MEMBERS OF THE MEDIA AT A 1964 PRESS CONFERENCE DURING THE HEIGHT OF BEATLEMANIA.

**LEFT: JOHN LENNON AND HIS SON JULIAN PREPARE TO BOARD A PLANE FOR GREECE IN JULY 1967.**

**THIS PAGE: JOHN LENNON AND WIFE YOKO ONO**

GEORGE HARRISON
AND RINGO STARR
ENJOYING THEIR
POST-BEATLES YEARS

PAUL McCARTNEY AND HIS LATE WIFE LINDA TAKE THE STAGE TOGETHER WITH THE MUSICAL GROUP WINGS.

MUSIC LEGENDS WILLIE NELSON AND RINGO STARR SHARE THE STAGE AT THE 34TH ANNUAL GRAMMY AWARDS IN 1992.

PAUL McCARTNEY, STING AND ERIC CLAPTON (FROM LEFT TO RIGHT) AND STING PERFORM IN THE ROYAL ALBERT HALL AS PART OF THE "AID FOR MONTSERRAT" CONCERT IN 1997.

PAUL McCARTNEY
IN CONCERT
IN 1999

OPPOSITE PAGE, TOP: FORMER BEATLES RINGO STARR AND GEORGE HARRISON ATTEND THE CHELSEA FLOWER SHOW IN 1999.

OPPOSITE PAGE, BOTTOM: RINGO STARR, PAUL McCARTNEY, GEORGE HARRISON AND PRODUCER GEORGE MARTIN (FROM LEFT TO RIGHT) AT LONDON'S ABBEY ROAD STUDIOS IN THE MID-1990S.

THIS PAGE, TOP LEFT: MUSIC LEGENDS BOB DYLAN AND GEORGE HARRISON
THIS PAGE, LOWER LEFT: GEORGE HARRISON AND MADONNA
THIS PAGE, RIGHT: RINGO STARR RELAXES BETWEEN SCENES OF 'CAVEMAN: THE MOVIE.'

LINDA AND PAUL
McCARTNEY

YOKO ONO AND JOHN LENNON GIVE PEACE A CHANCE.

# THE BEATLES'

*Editor's note: Numbers in parentheses signify the highest point a single reached on the Billboard magazine pop music chart.*

Album Title: **Introducing the Beatles**
Release Date: July 22, 1963
Produced By: George Martin
Label: Vee Jay
Singles: I Saw Her Standing There (#1), Love Me Do (#1) w/ P.S. I Love You, Twist and Shout (#2), Do You Want to Know a Secret (#2)

Album Title: **Meet the Beatles**
Release Date: January 20, 1964
Produced By: George Martin
Label: Capitol
Singles: I Want To Hold Your Hand (#1) w/ I Saw Her Standing There

Album Title: **The Beatles' Second Album**
Release Date: April 10, 1964
Produced By: George Martin
Label: Capitol
Singles: Thank You Girl (#2), She Loves You (#1)

Album Title: **A Hard Day's Night**
Release Date: June 26, 1964
Produced By: George Martin
Label: United Artists
Singles: A Hard Day's Night (#1) w/ I Should Have Known Better (instrumental), I'll Cry Instead (#25), Can't Buy Me Love (#11)

Album Title: **Something New**
Release Date: July 20, 1964
Produced By: George Martin
Label: Capitol
Singles: I'll Cry Instead (#25), Slow Down (#17) w/ Matchbox, And I Love Her (#12), If I Fell (#12)

Album Title: **The Beatles' Story**
Release Date: November 23, 1964
Produced By: Gary Usher and Roger Christian
Label: Capitol
Note: This album includes a collection of interviews and music exploring the Beatlemania phenomenon.

Album Title: **Beatles '65**
Release Date: December 15, 1964
Produced By: George Martin
Label: Capitol
Singles: She's a Women (#1), I Feel Fine (#1).

Album Title: **The Early Beatles**
Release Date: March 22, 1965

Produced By: George Martin
Label: Capitol
Singles: Please Please Me (#3), Twist and Shout (#2), Love Me Do (#1)

Album Title: **Beatles VI**
Release Date: June 14, 1965
Produced By: George Martin
Label: Capitol
Singles: Eight Days a Week (#1) w/ I Don't Want To Spoil the Party, Yes It Is (#1)

Album Title: **Help!** *(Original Soundtrack Album)*
Release Date: August 13, 1965
Produced By: George Martin
Label: Capitol
Singles: Help! (#1), Ticket to Ride (#1)

Album Title: **Rubber Soul**
Release Date: December 6, 1965
Produced By: George Martin
Label: Capitol
Singles: I've Just Seen a Face, Norwegian Wood (This Bird Has Flown), Michelle

Album Title: **"Yesterday"... And Today**
Release Date: June 20, 1966
Produced By: George Martin
Label: Capitol
Singles: Nowhere Man ( #3), Yesterday (#1) w/ Act Naturally, We Can Work It Out (#1) w/ Day Tripper

Album Title: **Revolver**
Release Date: August 8, 1966
Produced By: George Martin
Label: Capitol
Singles: Eleanor Rigby (#2), Yellow Submarine (#2)

Album Title: **Sgt. Pepper's Lonely Hearts Club Band**
Release Date: June 2, 1967
Produced By: George Martin
Label: Capitol
Singles: Sgt. Pepper's Lonely Hearts Club Band (#72) w/ With a Little Help From My Friends

Album Title: **Magical Mystery Tour**
Release Date: November 27, 1967
Produced By: George Martin
Label: Capitol
Singles: I Am the Walrus (#1) w/ Hello Goodbye, Strawberry Fields Forever (#1),
Penny Lane (#1), Baby You're a Rich Man (#1), All You Need Is Love (#1)

Album Title: **The Beatles** (White Album)
Release Date: November 25, 1968
Produced By: George Martin
Label: Apple
Singles: Ob-La-Di, Ob-La-Da (#49)

Album Title: **Yellow Submarine** (Original Soundtrack Album)
Release Date: January 13, 1969
Produced By: George Martin
Label: Apple
Singles: Yellow Submarine (#2), All You Need Is Love (#1)

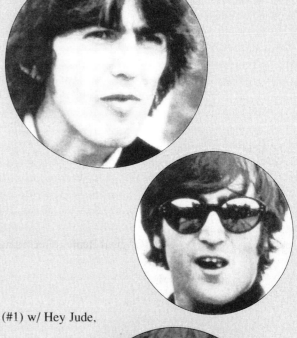

Album Title: **Abbey Road**
Release Date: October 1, 1969
Produced By: George Martin
Label: Apple
Singles: Come Together (#1) w/ Something

Album Title: **Hey Jude** (also called The Beatles Again)
Release Date: February 26, 1970
Produced By: George Martin
Label: Apple
Singles: Paperback Writer (#1) w/ Rain, Lady Madonna (#4), Revolution (#1) w/ Hey Jude,
Don't Let Me Down (#1), The Ballad of John and Yoko (#8)

Album Title: **The Beatles - Circa 1960 - In the Beginning**
Release Date: May 4, 1970
Produced By: George Martin
Label: Polydor
Singles: My Bonnie (#26)

Album Title: **Let It Be** (Original Soundtrack Album)
Release Date: May 18, 1970
Produced By: George Martin
Label: Apple
Singles: Let It Be (#1), The Long and Winding Road (#1) w/ For You Blue, Get Back (#1)

Album Title: **The Beatles' Christmas Album**
Release Date: July 22, 1963
Produced By: George Martin and The Beatles
Label: Apple
Note: This album was issued to U.S. members of *The Official Beatles Fan Club.*

Album Title: **The Beatles/1962-1966** (Red Album)
Release Date: April 2, 1973
Produced By: George Martin
Label: Apple

Singles: Double disc includes past hits Love Me Do (#1), Can't Buy Me Love (#1), Day Tripper (#1), We Can Work It Out (#1), Eleanor Rigby (#2), etc.

Album Title: **The Beatles/1967-1970** *(Blue Album)*
Release Date: April 2, 1973
Produced By: George Martin, and Disc Two tracks 13 (Hey Jude) and 14 (Revolution) by Phil Spector
Label: Apple
Singles: Double disc includes past hits Strawberry Fields Forever (#1), With a Little Help From My Friends (#72), I Am the Walrus (#1), Come Together (#1), Let It Be (#1), etc.

Album Title: **Rock 'N' Roll Music**
Release Date: June 7, 1976
Produced By: George Martin except Get Back, produced by George Martin and Phil Spector
Label: Capitol
Singles: Got To Get You Into My Life (#7), Get Back (#1), Revolution (#1).

Album Title: **The Beatles at the Hollywood Bowl**
Release Date: May 4, 1977
Produced By: Voyle Gilmore (Original Remote Recording), George Martin (Final Mixdown and Sequencing)
Label: Capitol
Singles: Ticket to Ride (#1), A Hard Day's Night (#1).

Album Title: **The Beatles Live! At the Star Club in Hamburg, Germany, 1962**
Release Date: June 13, 1977
Produced By: Larry Grossberg
Label: Lingasong
Singles: Double disc includes Roll Over Beethoven, Hippy Hippy Shake, Long Tall Sally, Remember You

Album Title: **Love Songs**
Release Date: October 21, 1977
Produced By: George Martin (except The Long and Winding Road by Phil Spector and George Martin)
Label: Capitol
Singles: Something (#1), Yesterday (#1), If I Fell (#12)

Album Title: **The Beatles Collection** *(13 LP Boxed Set)*
Release Date: December 1, 1978
Produced By: George Martin and Phil Spector (LP 12)
Label: Capitol
Note: LP One: Please Please Me, LP Two: With The Beatles, LP Three: A Hard Day's Night, LP Four: Beatles For Sale, LP Five: Help!, LP Six: Rubber Soul, LP Seven: Revolver, LP Eight: Sgt. Pepper's Lonely Hearts Club Band, LP Nine: The Beatles, LP Ten: Yellow Submarine, LP Eleven: Abbey Road, LP Twelve: Let It Be, Bonus LP: Rarities

Album Title: **Rarities**
Release Date: March 24, 1980
Produced By: George Martin
Label: Capitol
Singles: Love Me Do (#1), Helter Skelter, Misery

Album Title: ***Reel Music***
Release Date: March 22, 1982
Produced By: George Martin except tracks 12 (Let It Be), 13 (Get Back),
14 (The Long Winding Road) by Phil Spector
Label: Capitol
Note: Includes music from Beatles films such as A Hard Day's Night (#1),
Help! (#1) and Magical Mystery Tour

Album Title: ***The Complete Silver Beatles***
Release Date: September 27, 1982
Produced By: Mike Smith
Label: Audio Rarities
Singles: Three Cool Cats, Crying, Waiting, Hoping, Besame Mucho

Album Title: ***20 Greatest Hits***
Release Date: October 11, 1982
Produced By: George Martin, except track 20 (The Long Winding Road)
by George Martin (January 1970) and Phil Spector (March 1970)
Label: Capitol
Singles: I Want to Hold Your Hand (#1), Eight Days A Week (#1), Penny Lane (#1)

Album title: ***Past Masters Volume 1***
Release Date: March 7, 1988
Produced By: George Martin
Label: Capitol
Singles: Thank You Girl, Komm, Gib Mir Deine Hand

Album Title: ***Past Masters Volume 2***
Release Date: March 7, 1988
Produced By: George Martin
Label: Capitol
Singles: Day Tripper (#1), Hey Jude (#1)

Album Title: ***The Beatles Live at the B.B.C.***
Release Date: November 30, 1994
Produced By: George Martin
Label: Capitol
Note: Recorded Live March 1962, June 1965 double disc includes Too
Much Monkey Business, A Shot of Rhythm and Blues,
You Really Got a Hold on Me

Album Title: ***Anthology 1***
Release Date: November 21, 1995
Produced By: George Martin
Label: Capitol
Singles: Double disc includes Free As a Bird, Ain't She Sweet
(#19), Money (That's What I Want)

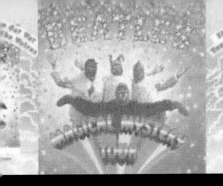

Album Title: **Anthology 2**
Release Date: March 19, 1996
Produced By: George Martin
Label: Capitol
Singles: Double disc includes Yes It Is (#1), Yesterday (#1),
Lady Madonna (#4), Penny Lane (#1)

Album Title: **Anthology 3**
Release Date: October 29, 1996
Produced By: George Martin
Label: Capitol
Singles: Double disc includes Ob-La-Di, Ob-La-Da (#49),
While My Guitar Gently Weeps, Julia, Ain't She Sweet (#19)

Album Title: **Yellow Submarine Soundtrack**
Release Date: September 14, 1999
Produced By: George Martin
Label: Capitol
Singles: Nowhere Man (#3), Baby You're a Rich Man (#1), All You Need Is
Love (#1)

*Unfinished Music No.1: Two Virgins*, Apple/Tetragrammation, November 11, 1968
*Unfinished Music No.2: Life With The Lions*, Apple, May 26, 1969
*Wedding Album*, Apple, October 20, 1969
*The Plastic Ono Band-Live Peace In Toronto 1969*, Apple, December 12, 1969
*John Lennon/Plastic Ono Band,* Apple, December 11, 1970
*Imagine,* Apple, September 9, 1971
*Sometime in New York City*, Apple, June 12, 1972
*Mind Games*, Apple, November 2, 1973
*Wall and Bridges*, Apple, September 26, 1974
*Rock 'N' Roll*, Apple, February 17, 1975
*Shaved Fish*, Apple, October 24, 1975
*Double Fantasy*, Geffen, November 15, 1980
*The John Lennon Collection*, Geffen, November 8, 1982
*Milk and Honey*, Polydor, January 19, 1984
*Live in New York City*, Capitol, January 24, 1986
*MenLove Ave.*, Capitol, October 27, 1986
*Imagine: John Lennon* (Music From The Original Motion Picture), Capitol,
October 4, 1988
*Lennon* (4 CD Boxed Set), Capitol, October 30, 1990
*Lennon Legend: The Very Best of John Lennon*, Parlophone, February 24, 1998
*John Lennon Anthology* (4 CD Boxed Set), Capitol, November 3, 1998
*Wonsaponatime*, Capitol, November 3, 1998

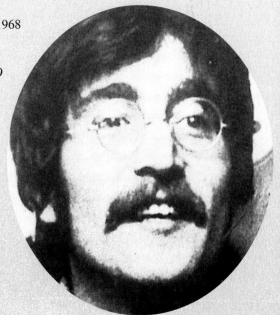

*The Family Way (Original Soundtrack Album)*, London, June 12, 1967
*McCartney*, Apple, April 20, 1970
*RAM*, Apple, May 17, 1971
*Wild Life* (Wings Album), Apple, December 7, 1971
*Red Rose Speedway* (Wings Album), Apple, April 30, 1973
*Band On the Run* (Wings Album), Apple, December 5, 1973
*Venus and Mars* (Wings Album), Capitol, May 27, 1975
*Wings at the Speed of Sound* (Wings Album), Capitol, March 25, 1976
*Wings Over America* (Wings Album), Capitol, December 10, 1976
*Thrillington*, Capitol, May 17, 1977
*London Twist* (Wings Album), Capitol, March 31, 1978
*Wings Greatest* (Wings Album), Capitol, November 27, 1978
*Back to the Egg* (Wings Album), Columbia, June 11, 1979
*McCartney II*, Columbia, May 26, 1980
*Tug of War*, Columbia, April 26, 1982
*Pipes of Peace*, Columbia, October 31, 1983
*Give My Regards to Broad Street*, Columbia, October 22, 1984
*Press to Play*, Capitol, August 22, 1986
*All the Best*, Capitol, December 5, 1987
*Flowers in the Dirt*, Capitol, June 6, 1989
*Tripping the Live Fantastic*, Capitol, November 6, 1990
*Tripping the Lice Fantastic-Highlights*, Capitol, November 20, 1990
*Paul McCartney Unplugged (the Official Bootleg)*, Capitol, June 4, 1991
*Paul McCartney's Liverpool Oratorio*, EMI Classics, October 22, 1991
*Choba B CCP (The Russian Album)*, Capitol, October 29, 1991
*Off The Ground*, Capitol, February 9, 1993
*Paul is Life*, Capitol, November 16, 1993
*Strawberries Oceans Ships Forest*, Capitol, February 22, 1994
*Flaming Pie, Capitol*, May 27, 1997
*Paul McCartney's Standing Stone*, EMI Classics, September 23, 1997
*Rushes*, EMI/Capitol, October 20, 1998
*Run Devil Run*, Capitol, October 5, 1999
*Working Classical*, EMI Classics, October 19, 1999

*Wonderwall (Original Soundtrack Album)*, Apple, December 2, 1968
*Electronic Sound*, Apple, May 26, 1969
*All Things Must Pass*, Apple, November 27, 1970
*The Concert For Bangladesh*, Apple, December 20, 1971
*Living In The Material World*, Apple, May 30, 1973
*Dark Horse*, Apple, December 9, 1974
*Extra Texture-Read All About It*, Apple, September 22, 1975
*The Best of George Harrison*, Capitol, November 8, 1976
*Thirty Three & 1/3*, Dark Horse, November 24, 1976
*George Harrison*, Dark Horse, February 20, 1979
*Somewhere In England*, Dark Horse, June 1, 1981
*Gone Troppo*, Dark Horse, November 8, 1982
*Cloud Nine*, Dark Horse, November 2, 1987
*Traveling Wilburys Vol. 1*, Wilbury, October 25, 1988
*Best of Dark Horse 1976-1989*, Dark Horse/Warner Bros., October 9, 1989
*Traveling Wilburys Vol. 3*, Wilbury/Warner Bros., October 29, 1990
*George Harrison Live in Japan*, Warner Bros./Dark Horse, July 10, 1992

Sentimental Journey, Apple, April 24, 1970
Beaucoups of Blues, Apple, September 28, 1970
Ringo, Apple, November 2, 1973
Goodnight Vienna, Apple, November 18, 1974
Blast From Your Past, Apple, November 20, 1974
Ringo's Rotogravure, Atlantic, September 27, 1976
Ringo the 4th, Atlantic, September 26, 1977
Bad Boy, Portrait, April 17, 1978
Stop and Smell the Roses, Boardwalk, October 26, 1981
Old Wave, RCA (Canada), June 24, 1983
Starr Struck: Best of Ringo Starr Vol. 2, Rhino, March 1, 1989
Ringo Starr and His All-Starr Band, Rykodisc, October 16, 1990
Time Takes Time, Private, May 22, 1992
Ringo Starr and His All-Starr Band: Live From Montreux,
Rykodisc, October 1, 1993
Ringo Starr and His Third All-Starr Band: Vol.1,
Blockbuster Exclusive, August 12, 1997
Vertical Man, Mercury, June 16, 1998
VH1 Storytellers, Mercury, October 20, 1998
I Wanna Be Santa Claus, Mercury, October 19, 1999

# THE BEATLES'

Name: **A Hard Day's Night**
Release Date: July 6, 1964
Producer: Walter Shenson
Director: Richard Lester
Starring: The Beatles, Wilfrid Brambell,
Norman Rossington, Victor Spinetti,
John Junkin

Name: **Help!**
Release Date: July 29, 1965
Producer: Walter Shenson
Director: Richard Lester
Starring: The Beatles, Leo McKern,
Eleanor Bron, Victor Spinetti, Roy Kinnear

Name: *Magical Mystery Tour*
Release Date: December 26, 1967
Producer: The Beatles
Director: The Beatles
Starring: The Beatles, Jessie Robbins,
Ivor Cutler, Derek Royle, Mandy Weet,
Victor Spinetti

Name: **Yellow Submarine**
Release Date: July 17, 1968
Producer: Al Brodax
Director: George Duning
Starring: The voices of The Beatles, John Clive,
Geoffrey Hughes, Paul Angelis,
Dick Emery, Lance Percival and Peter Batten.

Name: **Let It Be**
Release Date: May 13, 1970
Producer: Mal Evans
Director: Michael Lindsay-Hogg
Starring: The Beatles, Yoko Ono,
Billy Preston, Mal Evans

Name: **The Beatles Anthology**
Release Date: November 19, 1995
Producers: Neil Aspinall and Chips Chipperfield
Directors: Bob Smeaton and Geoff Wonfor
Starring: The Beatles, Neil Aspinall,
George Martin, Derek Taylor

# THE BEATLES